The UNSINKABLE Mrs. BROWN

The UNSINKABLE *Mrs.* BROWN

CAROLINE BANCROFT

*Illustrated with photographs from
The Denver Post,
The Denver Public Library, and
The State Historical Society*

BOWER
HOUSE

DENVER

Cover Design and Illustration by Margaret McCullough

Library of Congress Cataloging-inPublication Data on file.

A NOTE FROM THE PUBLISHER

The history of Colorado is the stuff of legend—full of bandits and fortune-seekers, treasure found and lost, racy madams and reclusive miners, all set in the beautiful and brutal Rocky Mountains. These stories are part of the American heritage; they are part of who we are and how we dream. They inspire the kind of books we publish at Bower House, like the titles by Caroline Bancroft in our Little Western Library series.

These books are old—in fact *The Unsinkable Mrs. Brown* was among the first biographies of "Molly" Brown ever written—but these books are worth reviving because the lore in them is truly timeless and they hit the bulls-eye of our mission. No one matches the wit and power of Caroline Bancroft; former president of the Colorado Folklore Society, she is the original, definitive voice of the Centennial State. An intriguing character herself, Bancroft writes her brief histories and biographies as if she were sitting on a log next to you, firelight sparkling in her eyes, a tin cup of hot cowboy coffee in her hand, spinning her tales with wit and authority.

Perfect for Colorado natives and newcomers alike, the Little Western Library series is a must-have for lovers of the mountains and of the people who made Colorado one of the most intriguing states in the nation. *Collect them all:*

The Unsinkable Mrs. Brown

Colorado's Lost Goldmines & Buried Treasure

Silver Queen: The Fabulous Story of Baby Doe Tabor

Six Racy Madams of Colorado

ACKNOWLEDGMENTS
Reprinted from the first edition

For Research Aid:
Without the generous help of Lorena Jones and Allen Young of *The Denver Post* and the understanding staff of the Western History Department of the Denver Public Library—Ina T. Aulls, Alys Freeze, Opal Harber and Katherine Hawkins—this booklet could not have been written. Numerous others have helped, including Walter Lord, author of "A Night to Remember," the staffs of the Lake County and Pitkin County Court Houses, Agnes Wright Spring, official Colorado Historian, J. R. Morrison of the *Louisiana Press-Journal*, Missouri; Charles Wiseman, Mary Gibbs King, Kenneth C. Botkin, John Winkler, E. L. Sparks of the *Courier Post*, the Reverend Jerry W. Mahoney, Mrs. Joe Denkler, Mrs. John O'Hearn, Miss Wiseman, Mrs. Norman Dean Frost, Mrs. Albert Frier, Mary Clune and Mrs. Anne Gibson, all of Hannibal, Missouri; Mr. and Mrs. E. L. Brown, Mrs. Marian (Poppy) Smith and Reverend E. L. Horgan of Leadville, Colorado; Mrs. Ernest W. Dunning, Mrs. Frank H. Ricketson, Jr., Frank McLister, Mrs. Robert Archibold, Mrs. Horace Bennett, and Edwin Darby of Denver; Ella Grable of Arvada; Joseph M. Bryant of New York; Emil Jemail of the Daily News, Rose Weisberg and Louise Cottrell of Newport, Rhode Island; Mrs. Ernest Shaw and Mrs. Henry F. Coe of Cody, Wyoming, and Lola Homsher, Wyoming State Archivist. Still many more than these have supplied aid, whose names I shall hope to mention in the event I complete a full size biography of Mrs. J. J. Brown.

For Photographs:
The Denver Post, The Denver Public Library, Mrs. E. L. Brown, Mrs. Anne Gibson, Mary Clune, Charles Wiesman, Mrs. Ernest W. Dunning and Mrs. Ella Grable supplied the photographs relating to Mrs. Brown; Mr. and Mrs. Josiah Holland, the one of the Sacred Thirty Six. John Winkler, Kenneth Botkin and J. R. Morrison supplied Hannibal photographs. The Division of State Archives of the Colorado Historical Society supplied prints of W. H. Jackson negatives of Leadville subjects through the courtesy of Mrs. Dolores Renze. Robert Vaughan of Perth, Ontario, loaned the negatives of photos of his Carpathia medal. Mrs. Ernest Shaw gave me a picture of her daughter, Peg, a duplicate of one carried by Mrs. Brown. My gratitude to all.

For Criticism:
Marian Castle, author of the Colorado novel, "Roxana," has graciously read the script to make suggestions for improvement of the style.

For Proofreading:
Miss Anne Matlock and Mrs. J. Alvin Fitz ell donated time for catching typographical errors, the tedious chore that only generous friends would perform.

The Author

Caroline Bancroft was a third generation Coloradan who began her literary career by joining the staff of *The Denver Post* in 1928. For five years she edited a book page and wrote historical features for the Sunday edition. On a travel assignment for the *New York Evening Post*, she interviewed a long list of celebrated authors in New York, London, Paris, Holland, and India. Her articles have appeared in many nationally known magazines.

Her long-standing interest in western history was inherited. Her pioneer grandfather, Dr. F. J. Bancroft (after whom the three-crested, Continental Divide peak just south of James is named), was a founder of the Colorado Historical Society and its first president for seventeen years. Her father, George J. Bancroft, a mining engineer, wrote many mining and reclamation contributions to the growing body of Colorado lore.

Caroline Bancroft has carried on the family tradition. A Bachelor of Arts from Smith College, she later obtained a Master of Arts degree from the University of Denver, writing her thesis on Central City, Colorado. She taught Colorado history at Randell School in Denver and was the author of the intensely interesting series of Bancroft Booklets about Colorado, including *Unique Ghost Towns and Mountain Spots, Denver's Lively Past, Augusta Tabor, Tabor's Matchless Mine and Lusty Leadville, Famous Aspen, Six Racy Madams, The Unsinkable Mrs. Brown* and the extremely popular *Colorful Colorado.*

Edwin C. Johnson,
Governor of Colorado
1931-37, 1955-57

MAGGIE'S HAPPIEST TIME WAS IN LEADVILLE

The J. J. Brown family posed in 1891 against a typical background of the 'nineties. The setting was very likely their own house on Seventh Street and not that of a photographer's studio since Maggie loved to have all her possessions recorded. Late in life "The Unsinkable Mrs. Brown" would look back to these days and admit that money had never brought her happiness. She would add that her greatest nostalgia was for Leadville when her children were little.

Molly Brown Goes Marching on-

This booklet first appeared seven years ago. What I have to say now, in the spring of 1963, is in the nature of a few afterthoughts. What a strange story has transpired!

Several months before my booklet was published, Walter Lord had successfully recounted the events surrounding the sinking of the S. S. Titanic. His book *A Night To Remember* had separated the truth from the myths of that ship's incredible story. Among other revaluations Mr. Lord dealt rather fully with Mrs. J. J. Brown's actual role in the #6 lifeboat. He also referred to the ensuing myth of her running the boat while she stood in her corset and brandished a revolver—strictly nonsense, of course.

My own version of this incident had already been written at the time Mr. Lord's appeared. In essence my view varied hardly at all from his. But his was more detailed, and I elaborated my version with some of his thorough research before the booklet appeared. That dramatic night and the following days on the S. S. Carpathia seemed to me the high point in the biography of Margaret Tobin Brown. They still do.

The general public thought otherwise. People were interested in her social climbing struggle, artificial and spurious though that struggle was. Perhaps the public did not discern that despite minor triumphs Maggie Brown was never really "in." Although she obtained some sporadic acceptance here and abroad, much of her vaunted success was fantasy.

Yet the story had appeal and led to the production of a musical comedy with Tammy Grimes in the lead. *The Unsinkable Molly Brown* opened in New York in November, 1960, and became a great hit. The name, Molly Brown, was blazoned on a marquee no doubt to the infinite delight of its owner who had tried so hard and unsuccessfully, while she was alive, to have people call her Molly rather than Maggie. After running on Broadway for over a year, the musical toured across the nation and awakened considerable interest in the truth behind Mrs. Brown's story.

I was bombarded with questions. How much of the musical was legend, fiction and exaggeration? Was this or that episode really true? Did Maggie and Jim Brown (called Johnny in the musical) really make up their bitter and well-publicized differences?

In truth, there was only a modicum of history in the script, and the Browns were never reconciled. So let us revert.

1

Slightly over thirty years ago, on October 25, 1932, Mrs. J. J. Brown died. Except in Denver and Leadville her obituaries were meagre and inaccurate. The meagreness would have distressed her (but not the inaccuracies) for Maggie loved publicity. She had cultivated newspaper coverage and newspaper people in an era that frowned on both. People in society thought her actions vulgar. On the other hand many newspaper people liked her and defended her attitude. That was how she became a legend in her own time.

The legend was materially abetted in the year after her death by the publication of *Timberline* by Gene Fowler, a former Denver newspaperman. The main body of the highly spiced book was devoted to *The Denver Post* and its colorful owners. Thrown in with no relevance was a chapter on *The Unsinkable Mrs. Brown*. It was erroneous in the extreme, being largely tall tales of Fowler's own invention. Nonetheless the *Reader's Digest* ran the chapter as fact, and Fowler sold the movie rights of the whole book to Metro-Goldwyn-Mayer.

Years later, after the success of the musical comedy, the *Reader's Digest* reran the chapter in their French edition. They had planned to use it in all their editions and in the course of reworking, phoned me from New York to ask how Mrs. Brown received her Legion of Honor.

"In a hock shop," I answered.

They were startled, and likely did not believe me. Both Gene Fowler's and Maggie Brown's stories were so much more piquant than the truth.

The success of *Timberline* led Eastern publishers to look for other Western biographies. Two years later (in 1935) I was approached with an offer to write a biography, *The Unsinkable Mrs. Brown*, and I started to do research.

Many difficulties developed. Although I knew of Fowler's propensity to exaggerate and had not expected to find truth in his telling, I did expect quantities of old newspaper stories about Mrs. Brown to check out. Many did not. Documented records were scarce and other reliable sources proved almost impossible to find.

The most formidable difficulty was the attitude of her son, Lawrence P. Brown, a Leadville resident, who alternated between a desire to see his mother immortalized and panic that a serious writer would expose the truth. Since the little research already done on my part had revealed that the facts were far from the legend, the project was dropped. Neither the publisher nor I was interested in a glamorous whitewash job although we agreed that if further material came to light of a substantial nature, we might reconsider.

In 1949 Larry Brown died, survived by his second wife but estranged from his children who lived in California with his divorced first wife. "The Unsinkable" had always refused to meet the second wife and had quarreled bitterly with her son both on the score of his remarriage and Jim Brown's estate. Larry's passing was noted only as it tied in to his mother's story. He had had some of his mother's charm and of his father's taste for alcohol but none of his parents' enterprise. He lived out his life, dabbling in various mining schemes and sometimes "conning" other people into financing them. Mostly he subsisted on a small income from inherited wealth.

His sister, Helen, had made a fine marriage in the East, raised two sons who did well, and was devoted to her grandchildren. She had put her Western past completely away, had no interest in Colorado, and had dropped all of her Denver friends. Helen disliked publicity as much as her "unsinkable" mother loved it. She preferred to have everything about her mother forgotten. Helen wanted neither the myth nor the truth perpetuated.

The years passed. From time to time I added to my researches on Mrs. J. J. Brown, mostly out of curiosity, that compelling force which makes historians search for the underlying truth. More data was gleaned in Denver, Leadville, Hannibal, Newport and New York. Soon I was the only quasi-authority on her life.

In 1955 the American Telephone Company was sponsoring a TV series of biographies, narrated by John Nesbitt and produced by the Hal Roach Studios. I received a long distance call from Hollywood. The director, Jerry Stagg, wanted me to supply a script on Maggie Brown.

I dug out my reams of notes and sat down at the typewriter. The resulting script, although considerably altered, was eventually produced and in February, 1957, shown nationally. While I was working on the TV assignment, I decided to set down a short biography and leave the decision of Maggie Brown's worth as a full length subject to some later date. That day has never arrived.

Now it has been announced that toward October of this year, 1963, Metro-Goldwyn-Mayer will proceed with a movie. It is to be based in large part on the musical comedy *The Unsinkable Molly Brown*. Debbie Reynolds is scheduled to play the role created on the stage by Tammy Grimes. Background shots, if not the whole movie, are supposed to be shot in Colorado. Once again Maggie Brown will attain the limelight. And so the legend grows and grows.

How happy Margaret Tobin Brown must be! For all time she will be remembered as the lady of a great romance and as the heroine of an internationally known success story. More than that, her name lives as Molly (so upper class) and not Maggie (which all her family and friends called her—drat them!)

No matter if neither the romance nor the success story is true. Posthumously she has attained her dreamed-of pinnacle.

3

THE SACRED THIRTY-SIX

Denver's inner society circle is seen dining at the Country Club at a crepe paper ball. Every dress in the room is made out of crepe paper with the exception of Mrs. Crawford Hill's. She is seated at far right with a large corsage on her shoulder; the date about 1910.

4

The Unsinkable Mrs. Brown

She Was Snubbed by The Sacred Thirty-Six
But Was Not Sunk

Margaret Tobin of Hannibal, Missouri, was a high-spirited, bosomy Irish girl whose wavy auburn hair crowned a head alive with ambition. She was the daughter of a ditchdigger for the gas works, John Tobin. But, as Maggie looked about her at the thriving, noisy rail-and-riverboat center, she dreamed of greater things than the life of a laborer's daughter. She did not look as often at the river boats as she did at the puffing steam engines that pulled out of the high-towered ornate railroad depot. Every one of Hannibal's five railroads had a direct line or a feeder that chugged off to the West, land of gold, silver and untold riches.

Born in July, 1867, Maggie had some public school education which did not take very well. Maggie was always too busy being a tomboy and playing with her older brother's gang. His name was Daniel, and she was especially fond of him. In her day-dreams, she pictured him as rising to a high place in the world.

Early in 1880 when Maggie was twelve and Dan was sixteen, he had a job selling newspapers on a railway car. Their mother thought this was already a step up for her brilliant son, since she could neither read nor write. But Maggie was contemptuous. She pictured the day when Dan would have a private car which would in turn be hooked on each one of the trains which steamed away from Hannibal's feudal-castle depot.

Maggie also had two older half-sisters, since her father, a widower with a daughter, Katie, by a previous marriage, had married a widow, Johanna Collins, with a daughter, Mary Ann. These girls eventually became Mrs. John A. Becker of Hannibal, and Mrs. John Laundrigan of Leadville, and later Aspen, Colorado, and finally assorted residences in Nevada. Besides Daniel, there were a full sister and brother, Ellen and William, who were younger than Maggie. Ellen had a colorful career as a sought-after beauty whose last marriage was to the Baron von Reitzenstein of Bavaria, Germany. The six children always remained close and in later years made many visits to each other's homes.

By the time that she was in her 'teens, Maggie was working in a tobacco

5

MAGGIE'S BIRTHPLACE IN HANNIBAL

This small frame house, dating from before the Civil War, looked like this in 1953. The Tobin family was frequently called "Shanty Irish."

factory and later as a waitress at the Park Hotel. Here, all the *bon ton* of the busy community dined and danced.

While serving table at the Park Hotel, Mark Twain made one of his trips back to his home town, and Maggie begged the manager to be permitted to wait on him. Mark Twain had gone west many years before and, while he had not acquired mining wealth, he did achieve fame. He was a celebrity and that was what Maggie envied, even more than riches.

He told her about the early Nevada and California camps and said that they were bringing in new finds throughout the Rockies all the time. Maggie's mind was made up—she would persuade Daniel to leave for the latest fabulous strike, the silver camp of Leadville, Colorado.

Daniel did leave, probably in 1883, shortly after John Laundrigan had set up as a blacksmith in Leadville, and the next year Maggie followed them. She finally accomplished her first goal—to chug out of the ornate station on her way west. It was the first time Maggie had been on a train. She had packed all of her belongings in a satchel and a carpet bag, and she carried enough food for three days, which her mother had carefully prepared. This was wrapped in shoe boxes.

When she arrived in Leadville, she found an even more boisterous community than Hannibal. It had been very wild and lawless three years

6

DENKLER'S ALLEY RUNS DOWNHILL

The Tobin house (at left) was at the corner of Prospect and Sixth, colloquially renamed. The hill in the distance is Mark Twain's Cardiff.

before. Now shootings were less frequent but the red-light houses, the variety halls and the saloons still made up the largest part of the business district.

Maggie went to stay at a boarding house on Fifth Street at the edge of town, just under the brow of the great Carbonate Hill that was making millionaires by the dozen. A stone's throw away the steam hoists were chugging, their whistles screeching, ore buckets were clanging, and a steady stream of ore wagons passed down Fifth Street, carrying their precious loads to the smelter. Daniel lived at the boarding house and worked at one of the mines up on the hill. Maggie got a job, tending table and helping to wash up.

Soon she was joking with the boarders and getting to know people up and down the street. Later she became a clerk in Daniels, Fisher and Smith's Emporium on Harrison Avenue. One day James J. Brown, manager of the Louisville mine, who went to work each day up Fifth Street and had seen Maggie picnicking with some friends on the hill, asked to meet her. Maggie was not much interested—she was seventeen years old and he was almost thirty. She thought he was an old man.

But Jim Brown plied his suit with acumen. He hired the best livery horses to take her driving and he talked to her about mining. He said he was investing in the mines he managed and that he was bound to strike it rich. After a continued courtship, she relented.

7

PLAYGROUND

The Tobin children roamed the many wooded hills around their thriving town. A favorite spot was Lover's Leap, shown here. Note the Mississippi river boat, a stern wheeler, setting out from shore in the waters far below the cliff. They're now gone.

They were married at the Church of the Annunciation in Leadville, September 1, 1886 and went to live in Stumptown. This was a log cabin and wood-shanty settlement about three miles east of Leadville, closer to Jim's mines. They lived in a two-room log cabin.

It was here that the myth started about Jim's making a rich strike, bringing her home a large sum of paper money to hide, of her putting it in the stove since it was a summer night, of Jim's going to town to celebrate and bringing home some cronies, of its being cold at 10,500 feet altitude, of his lighting a fire and burning up their fortune.

When Maggie discovered the loss, she burst into tears. But Jim comforted her with the remark:

"Never mind, darling, I'll make that much again for you—and more!"

At the time the story first became current the sum that Jim was supposed to have burnt up was $10,000. By 1953 when a columnist on the *Rocky*

8

Mountain News retold the story as gospel history, contemporary inflation had taken over. The sum was $300,000.

The truth is *no* paper money was ever used in a Colorado mining camp until after World War I. Paper money was strictly *infra dig*. The story, as told, is true except that the sum was from the petty cash box, that it was in gold and silver coin amounting to around $75, that it belonged to the company, and that they fished it out of the ashes after the fire had burned down. Maggie used to tell the story in early years and end up with: "Suppose it had been paper money!"

In 1925, when Maggie was staying at the Hotel Vendome during one of her frequent visits back to Leadville, Dolly Brown spoke to her about the story. Dolly was the wife of Edward Louis Brown, familiarly known as Ted. The young Browns were very close to the Jim Browns, and Ted was always referred to as Jim's nephew although actually he was the son of Jim's first cousin. Jim gave Ted a Regis College education in Denver and for many years employed the younger Brown as a secretary and rent collector for Denver real estate holdings.

Maggie was equally fond of them and often gave Dolly dresses she had tired of. They had many heart-to-heart talks in the course of a nearly twenty-year friendship, and Dolly was in a position to talk frankly.

"Aunt Maggie," Dolly said, "You know that isn't true about your hiding a fortune in the stove and it's getting burned up. Why don't you deny it?"

"Oh, hell, what difference does it make?" she replied. "It's a damn good story. And I don't care what the newspapers say about me, just so they say something."

But in the late 1880's no one was writing anything about Maggie or her astute husband. Without any dramatics, Jim Brown prospered as a mine superintendent. They moved into Leadville and bought a house on Seventh Street to raise two children, a boy, Lawrence, and a girl, Helen. They were friendly with the Sam Nicholsons who lived next door. Their sons, Lawrence Brown and Edward Nicholson (the latter, now public relations manager for the United Air Lines in Denver), became boon companions. But the Browns were unknown in Leadville's higher social and mining echelons. Then Jim did strike it rich in 1894 when he found gold, not silver, in the Little Jonny mine (note spelling). He did not own the mine but was employed by its owners as superintendent. Because of his successful management in finding and developing a gold area after the collapse of silver in the Panic of 1893, the grateful owners gave him one-eighth interest in the mine.

The Little Jonny very quickly began to pay fantastic dividends and, with this money, the Browns left their clapboard house in Leadville (where they had lived for six years) and moved to Denver. Here they bought a brownstone-with-granite-trim house at 1340 Pennsylvania Street. It had a

9

WHEN YOUNG, MAGGIE LONGED TO LEAVE

This castle of a busy railroad station was a principal shipping spot for the West. Today the ornate depot has gone and the town is asleep.

high parapet and wall to frame its approaching stone steps. This residence became known as the House of the Lions because Mrs. Brown decorated the wall with four carved lions, standing and sitting. (The house still stands and the two sitting lions remain.)

Maggie Brown set out to conquer Denver society. She had very little knowledge of money or manners. Her English was atrocious and gave birth to many a story, told with malicious glee at smart dinner parties. Actually Jim Brown had made, and was to make, only a million or two, and his fortune was always much less than many other Colorado and Denver millionaires of this period. But Maggie spent money as if she were married to a Croesus in an effort to make the social grade.

She acquired a country place and gave Denver society probably its best laugh when she wrote a letter to a local scandal sheet of those days, *Polly Pry*, explaining why she named her lodge, "Avoca." The item appeared thus:

MRS. J. J. BROWN EXPLAINS

Polly Pry and the readers of *Polly Pry* are very much indebted to Mrs. J. J. Brown for the following lucid and picturesque explanation of the hidden

LATER, HER SISTER'S HOME WAS A HAVEN

*Mag often visited her half-sister, Mrs. John Becker, at 322 North
Street and breakfasted on the back porch to watch the river shipping.*

meaning of the title of her Lodge—"Avoca, the Hand Made of the Lord"—
which we quote with scrupulous exactness.

Polly Pry:

Enclosed find the poem from which I have committed the sacrilege by
desecrating its title "Avoca" in applying it to a homestead in a valley of
Colorado. May I be pardoned of so grave a crime? If after leaving the
smelter smoke of Denver, travesing miles of uninteresting stretch of country,
in reaching the summit "behold" "the hand made of Lord," and the sublime
work of nature a panoramic view of a most picturesque valley bursts upon
me . . .

On my left are quartered the bravest of the brave, the bone and sinew
of our nation at Fort Logan on the other side spirals of a seat of knowledge
and wisdom Loretto Hights, with your vivid imagination can you form
mental picture of a place from a scenic standpoint more worthey of inspiring
the thought immortalized "Thomas Moor" in his sweet 'Vale of Avoca."

Truley yours,

September ninth   Margaret Tobin Brown
Thirteen forty Pennsylvania Avenue.   (Mrs. James J. Brown)

The "Sacred Thirty-Six," as Denver's top social crust was called, roared with laughter. For quite a few months, instead of being referred to as the "Impossible Mrs. Brown" by members of Denver society, she was called "The Hand Made of the Lord."

Snubbed repeatedly by those she tried to know, her ambition was undaunted. She hired tutors to teach her English, French, singing, elocution and deportment. She began to travel extensively to Europe and, by the turn of the century, around the world. This trip she later wrote up for one of the Denver newspapers.

Interspersed between her wide travels and strenuous studies, she returned to Denver to continue her assault on the Sacred Thirty-Six. Invitations to the Impossible Mrs. Brown's parties were ignored, and Maggie was forced to call in the neighborhood children to eat up her food.

A rather pathetic story of this period used to be told in later years by her son, Lawrence. One of the most elegant mansions of the time was the William Garrett Fisher house at 1600 Logan, about four blocks from Maggie's. It had been built in 1896 of Coal Creek lava stone and in the front had decorative lions carved of the same stone. Toward the north was an annex designed as art gallery, theatre and ballroom. Its walls were paneled in Argentine satin-wood that encased seven-foot high plate glass mirrors. Between each alternate mirrored panel hung paintings. The house, its owners and their friends represented everything for which Maggie longed.

W. G. Fisher died in April, 1897, and for several years the house was rented to William Cooke Daniels, son of W. B. Daniels who had been

DREAM REALIZED

The wedding breakfast for Mag and Jim was held at the Evergreen Lakes Hotel (shown at left) not far from Leadville. *T h e i r* honeymoon was spent at Twin Lakes, twenty miles away. Mag had been wed ten years in photo at right.

Fisher's partner in the smart Denver emporium, Daniels and Fisher's. The young Daniels couple were members of the Sacred Thirty-Six and did a lavish amount of chic entertaining.

One cold wintry night they were scheduled to give a house dance to which, needless to say, the Browns had not been invited. Maggie's heart was bursting with envy and curiosity. She suggested at the dinner table that she would like to stroll around and stand on the sidewalk to watch the guests arrive and study their ensembles. Jim scoffed at the idea—said he had never heard of anything so ridiculous.

When the meal was finished, Maggie asked Larry if he would go with her. He was about eleven at the time and delighted with an excuse to get out. He accepted; and his mother and he set out for the scene of revelry.

The house was surrounded by a tall fence of iron palings, supported by stone columns. It was possible to look directly through into the ballroom, seeing the guests a second time after having watched them alight from their carriages.

As the tedious cold quarters-of-an-hour passed, Larry hung so long on the iron paling fence that his hands and nose became congealed to the metal. He was tired and unhappy, and began to whimper. He asked his mother if they could not go home. But Maggie was enthralled and oblivious. She stayed on and on. Larry later said the intense longing and preoccupation, written on her face, made an indelible impression on him even though normally he was too young to be observant.

Another house that was close to Maggie's also piqued her curiosity. This mansion, now called Chappell House (a branch of the Denver Art Museum),

13

MAGGIE'S HAPPIEST YEARS WERE LIVED HERE

A two-room log cabin, the first one close to the Louisville mine and the second near the Little Jonny, were the young bride's first homes. This view shows the west side of Iron Hill, the little settlement of Graham Park at far left. Maggie's cabins looked like those at right.

was at 1300 Logan and had been built for his first wife in 1892 by the millionaire, Horace Wilson Bennett. The first Mrs. Bennett died; and in 1897 Julie Riche became the second Mrs. Bennett. Julie was highly cultivated, the daughter of French people who had given her a European education, and she made a gentle, well-mannered mistress for the large residence.

One day Mrs. Brown came to call. Julie received her in the little formal parlor to the right of the entrance which was a *bijou* of a room. It had gold brocade walls, gold furniture, an onyx fireplace with an exquisite French clock on the mantel and alabaster statues on onyx bases. Mrs. Brown was very impressed and told Julie she had been dying to get inside the house ever since she moved down from Leadville.

"How much did that cost?" Maggie demanded, pointing to the clock.

"I don't know," Julie replied. "You see, these things were bought for the first Mrs. Bennett. I was in school then and hadn't met my husband."

Maggie was undaunted. She kept on exclaiming and kept on asking the cost for each new piece of furnishing that caught her eye. She asked Julie to show her through the rest of the house. The young bride was a little appalled, but felt that out of deference to an older woman, she could but comply. The tour consisted of Maggie's whistling at intervals and asking the price, and Julie's reiterating that she did not know.

14

JIM MANAGED MANY FAMOUS SILVER MINES

*On the north end of Carbonate Hill were the Maid of Erin and the
Henriette mines (high with a trestle and below with a pipeline). The
group of buildings was tough Cletermore Gulch. The roads led into
Leadville; the first, with the ore wagon, down Fifth Street and home.*

A few weeks later Julie felt it only proper to return the call. She walked
the block distance and rang the bell. When there was no answer, she rang
several more times. Finally a little Irish woman, smoking a pipe, shuffled to
the door. Heartily, Maggie's mother invited the young bride in for a cup of
tea and ushered her back to the kitchen.

"Begorra, ye know Maggie won't let me smoke in the rest of the house,"
she explained. "And I like a bit of tobaccy with my tay."

The old Irish woman and the young French bride had a very sociable
time. They spent an hour in the kitchen while Mrs. Tobin regaled her visitor
with innumerable indiscreet family revelations, spoken in a pronounced
brogue and well-salted with "begorra's."

Mrs. Tobin told a story about how Jim and Maggie had decided to
raise chickens at Avoca and had ordered an incubator. They also had ordered
a new floor laid to make it weather-proof and warm for their new thorough-
bred poultry. The eggs in the incubator began to hatch. The chickens popped
out of the incubator too soon and all got stuck in the soft tar on the floor
where they struggled, cheeping lustily.

Mrs. Tobin swayed back in her rocker, laughing as lustily as the chickens
cheeped. But soon she was off again. Her next story was of the formal call

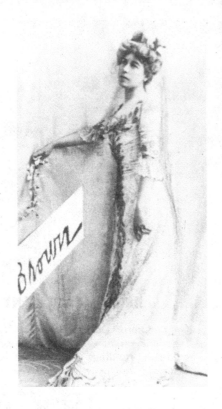

MAGGIE WAS PROUD OF HER EARLY BALL GOWNS

The photo to the right shows her in 1894, immediately after the Browns moved to Denver. At left she is shown in 1898, a gift to a friend.

the pious and proper Sisters of Loretto had made at the ranch, as they called Avoca.

They looked over the premises of the ranch and then politely inquired of Maggie:

"And what is Mr. Brown raising?"

"Nothing but straight Hell!" was her answer.

Mrs. Tobin was very sympathetic with Maggie's problems with Jim. He had always been inclined to drink too much, and now that he was rich he was getting involved with women of a more grasping nature than those of the Leadville parlor houses.

When Julie came to leave, Mrs. Tobin made her promise that she would never reveal to Maggie that the older woman had let her in and gossiped and visited with her in the kitchen. As Julie left, she could not help staring at the carved and painted Nubian slaves in the hall. Both were life-sized; one held out a tray for a card salver and the other acted as a newel-post light for the stairs (see photo in center spread). The two women parted pleasantly and Julie kept the secret until after Mrs. Tobin's death in 1905.

Along about this time Maggie developed her taste for expensive furs. She enjoyed parading down Seventeenth Street past the windows of the massive brownstone Denver Club in order to impress the distinguished oc-cupants who might be looking out. These men soon developed a by-word which they passed along to each other:

"Here comes Colorado's unique fur-bearing animal!"

None of Maggie's efforts seemed to impress people in the way she planned. She was no nearer her goal than when she was poor and uneducated in Leadville. She did, however, find a small place on committees for Catholic charities and threw her boundless vitality into organizing bazaars and raising money. The Catholic members of Denver society were very few in those days, and their position was too insecure to be much help to Maggie's climb up the social ladder. They accepted her executive ability and flair for pub-licity, rewarded her with a few unimportant invitations, and let it go at that.

Jim Brown regarded his wife's activities with an acrimonious eye when he was in town. He had opened a mining office, bought some Denver real estate (including the Colfax Hotel, opposite the mint, and several houses), and invested in mines in South Park, Creede, and other Colorado camps besides several in Arizona. Inevitably he traveled a great deal. But at home Jim liked simplicity as much as Maggie adored pretentiousness. He thought she ought to stay home, be a good mother and wife, and entertain their old friends, plain mining folks like themselves and their less well-off relatives. When Maggie would attempt one of her high-flown evening soirees, Jim would go down in the basement and sulk in the furnace room.

Quarrels between the two grew in intensity. Finally Jim's patience was tried to the utmost, although Denver regarded the episode as delightfully amusing and typical of Maggie. She was helping with a Catholic Fair, held on the then vacant lot at Colfax and Broadway, just across from the sweeping Capitol grounds. Maggie conceived the idea that some Indians, camping with their tepees on the green lawns of the state, would add to the publicity and attraction of the Fair.

The inimitable Mrs. Brown secured some peaceful Cheyennes who erected their tepees as she directed. But the legislators and governor were irate after the campers were installed, and ordered the Indians to pack up their belongings and be off. The Cheyennes loaded their tepees and miserable gear on their scrawny ponies to file up to the House of the Lions.

When Maggie heard the story of their predicament, she refused to be outdone by a few stuffy legislators.

17

HELEN AND LARRY WERE CHARMING YOUNGSTERS

Maggie's daughter was dressed in costume for a children's party in 1900. Larry was in the uniform of his Pennsylvania Military School.

"Hell, you can camp here," she said.

Accordingly the Indians pitched their tents on her front lawn and in her back yard and tethered their ponies in the elegant coach house alongside her Fritchle electric (which had recently displaced her brougham and matched team of horses).

The news soon spread about town, and droves of horseless carriages and smart turn-outs were driving up and down Pennsylvania Street to see what the Impossible Mrs. Brown was up to now. Gales of laughter greeted the Indians' squalor and filth.

At this juncture Jim Brown returned home. The sight appalled him He lost his Irish temper, packed his bag and left for Arizona, refusing to return. Undismayed Maggie made a huge success of the Fair, turned the money over to St. Joseph's hospital, rented the House of the Lions, and left for the East.

From that time on, although Jim Brown continued to support Maggie, they went their separate ways. Her path led her to cultural centers; his, to western mining camps. After a trip to Switzerland where Maggie learned to yodel, and a trip to Spain where she learned to play the guitar, she began to think of a cottage on Bellevue Avenue in Newport.

This desire grew out of a friendship she had struck up with the Countess Annie Leary, daughter of a Fifth Avenue hatter, who had had a papal title conferred on her by the Vatican. Maggie had come to know the countess in New York where both women were active in Catholic charity work, and the countess frequently spoke of her delightful summers on the elite island. The Leary house in Newport was called "Park Gate" and was at the corner of Pelham Street and Bellevue Avenue. It is now the Elks Club. The countess was a short, dumpy woman, not attractive in appearance but gracious in manner, provided that she was accorded full use of her title (about which she was very tenacious).

Countess Leary visited Maggie in Denver in June, 1910, and Maggie entertained for her several times. These included small parties in the House of Lions and a box party for the Walter Damrosch concert at the Civic Auditorium. The countess reciprocated with an invitation for Maggie and her daughter, Helen, now grown into a red-haired beauty, to visit her at Newport in July so that Helen might celebrate her twenty-first birthday in style. It was the success of that visit that crystallized Maggie's determination to rent a Newport house.

She first stayed at the Defossez Cottage, a boarding house, for short stays, but by 1913 she was installed at 44 Bellevue Avenue in a cottage she rented from Mrs. Aimee Reitz.

Maggie Brown had always had a dramatic sense and had tried her hand from time to time at amateur theatricals. During her first visits to Newport she put all her gifts together and was soon "the life of the party" wherever she was invited. Soon she became the vogue and began to appear on the swankiest lists sent out by the island colony, including those of the acknowledged dowager-leader, Mrs. O. H. P. Belmont.

Not long after she was calling Astors, Whitneys and Vanderbilts by their first names (or, as part of her clown act, by their last names with no title), and was accepted in New York as well as Newport. She had arrived; yet in the hidden recesses of her heart, which Maggie was in the habit of describing as being "as big as a ham," it still rankled that Denver society was not impressed. When its leaders crossed her trail in the capitals of Europe, they bowed coolly; and, if her name was brought to their attention by a titled personage or some established American, the Denverites smiled condescendingly and said:

"Of course, you don't know her the way we do."

The Denverites had a valid case in point. Maggie's soaring imagination

MAGGIE BROWN THREW A PARTY FOR DENVER SOCIETY IN 1910

A HUNGARIAN ORCHESTRA PLAYED ON THE PORCH

Maggie went all out to make her house-dance and garden party something that chic Denver would want to attend. She had tents erected on the lawn, furnished with oriental rugs and house furniture, and had the yard strung with hundreds of electric lights, sparkling beside Japanese lanterns. Outside and inside, potted shrubs and hundreds of dollars' worth of flowers turned the place into a gay bower.

LOHMAN'S DANCE BAND PLAYED INSIDE

Maggie thought her guests of honor should prove irresistible. They were the Baroness Helena von Reitzenstein (Ellen Tobin, her sister), Miss Flora Wilson of Washington and Miss Raghnilda Hobe, daughter of the Belgian Minister. The Sacred Thirty-Six ignored her invitation although lesser society came out of curiosity. Those who accepted never returned the indebtedness and continued to make fun of her.

GAY BLADE

Jim Brown liked quiet at home but was not an easy husband. He had a hot temper and a roving eye. He was sued for alienation of affection in 1903 and for $100,000 heart balm in 1919. Once he smashed the glass of the Fritchle electric in a family quarrel.

was leading her into some preposterous subterfuges. About this time she started telling Easterners that she was married to "Leadville Johnny" who had a fortune of twenty million dollars. She probably excused this fabrication on the score that it was a "good" story.

But "Leadville Johnny" was John F. Campion, principal owner of the Little Jonny mine, who had a fortune of probably five or six million and who had been one of Jim Brown's employers over a period of years. In any case he was many times richer than Jim Brown and was a much more important pioneer figure than Maggie's own husband. He had arrived in Leadville in April, 1879, at the height of the silver rush, when he was thirty years old, and soon became one of the "Cloud City's" most important citizens.

Jim Brown did not move to Leadville until 1885. He had come to know Eben Smith and David Moffat in a number of different mining camps, principally Aspen, where he sub-leased Horace Tabor's mine, the Tam O'Shanter, from Eben Smith. For ten years he worked as a manager and superintendent for mines owned or leased by Smith and Moffat, and it was through them that Jim came to know John Campion.

BARONESS

Ellen Tobin was born in June, 1871, and was the beauty of the family. Her hair was golden red. She moved to Leadville with her family after Maggie's marriage. She had a romantic life before marrying and divorced her first husband to wed an odd German baron.

John Campion, who was six years older than Jim, did not marry until 1895. The next year he moved to Denver and built his bride one of the most palatial mansions of the day at 800 Logan Street. The house (now the Red Cross) was a block east from the enormous columned residence of David Moffat, his friend and partner in many ventures. (David Moffat is remembered today mostly as the creator of the idea for a railroad tunnel under the continental divide—the Moffat Tunnel.)

The Campions had four children, born between 1896 and 1901, and soon began to take a prominent part in Catholic charities and civic organizations in Denver. But John Campion considered Leadville his real home, and the family retained a summer place at Twin Lakes until after his death. "Leadville Johnny" died in July, 1916, as the culmination of several years of failing health characterized principally by loss of sight.

In telling people that she was married to "Leadville Johnny," Maggie must have counted on the uninformed credulity of her listeners and on the fact that John Campion would never have a chance to read this amazing statement in print. After his death she apparently considered his widow and children

A SOCIETY QUEEN

*Mrs. Crawford Hill, leader of
The Sacred Thirty-Six, was a
southern belle, Louise Sneed,
who came to visit in Denver
at the Bethel castle on Colfax
Avenue which belonged to relatives. She married the only
son of Senator N. P. Hill
in 1895. On July 6, 1907 she
was presented at the court of
King Edward VII in the gown
shown here, much envied by
Maggie who longed to do
likewise. Mrs. Hill's velvet
train is in the State Museum.*

no threat to her claim. The "Leadville Johnny" fiction began to appear more frequently in print and has had a tenacious life ever since. It appeared in 1930 in *Fortune* magazine as part of an account of Maggie's life, and the fiction was still being repeated in 1955 when it appeared in an account of the sinking of the Titanic, called "Down to Eternity," a 35c paperback book.

Another of her fabrications centered around Mark Twain. As part of her dramatic performances with which she made her way up the social ladder in Newport, she sang, played the guitar, yodeled and gave recitations. At first these recitations were memorized poems, such as Service's "The Spell of the Yukon" or Chapman's "Out Where the West Begins," and formal selections for the elocutionist. But as time went on, Mag was called on more and more frequently to tell stories from her own life. She had a great flair for this, describing even the smallest episodes with wit and humor. She kept her audiences fascinated and enthralled with a true actress's gift for timing. When Mag found that this portion of her program made the greatest hit, she began to embellish the stories of her life. It was then that she laid the foundation for her own tale to compete with Calamity Jane or Annie Oakley.

AN ADVERTISEMENT

Although Maggie never succeeded in being presented at court, her tall tales turned her name into a legend even in her own lifetime. This photo and an apocryphal story were printed in many national magazines in the autumn of 1955 as an advertisement for United States Bonds. "Mrs. Brown refused to sink," said the ads which went on to add other exaggerated bits of her story. She may not have done what she said; but she gets credit.

Since Mag had adopted for herself a quasi-theatrical role, she decided to develop a more bizarre setting. She changed the name of the modest cottage that she was renting on the corner of Redwood Street and Bellevue Avenue to "Mon Etui." She built its dining-room over into a grotto. The center table was round and hollowed-out so that guests faced a fountain and rock-constructed aquarium that had tiny bridges, fernery-shaded paths and dripping waterfalls. The ceiling and walls of the room were hung with hunks of excelsior which Mag had dipped in brown plaster for a grotto effect.

In one corner of her living room she fitted up a sort of den arrangement which could also be used as a stage. This nook was hung with beads, draperies, scarfs and red lanterns and was Mag's idea of the perfect setting for her performances. To wait on her guests Mag found a short negro who was slightly deformed and whom she dressed as a Nubian slave, complete with silk turban, sash and full satin trousers. Her guests reported that the Nubian was completely devoted to Mag.

Against this background she liked to entertain at "An Evening with Molly Brown." (Mag came to think that her own nickname was not elegant

JAMES JOSEPH BROWN IN FORMAL POSES

The left was published in "Leadville, Lake County and the Gold Belt"
in 1895; the other, in 1911 in "Sketches of Colorado" by W. C. Ferril.

enough and increasingly she encouraged people to call her "Molly" or "Peggy.") The *piece de resistance* of such an evening was a lecture-reminiscence entitled, "My Relations with Mark Twain." She apparently decided that Hannibal was so far away and such an unimportant little hamlet that the truth of her one brief encounter with the celebrated writer would never catch up with her in dressy Newport.

In the lecture Mark Twain was a friend of her family's (despite the fact that he left Hannibal long before Maggie was born), and into this relationship she interlarded many homely little touches and humorous recollections. The climax of the lecture was a dramatic hurricane that caught Maggie in a small rowboat out on the Mississippi. Mark Twain jumped into the raging river and swam toward the overturned boat. (Hurricanes have not been recorded in that part of Missouri according to the weather bureau.) He saved the little girl's life.

During this period of Maggie's social climbing she developed a growing reverence for titles, genealogies, and all the trappings of the *Social Register*, *Burke's Peerage* and the *Almanach de Gotha*. She took her daughter, Helen, to England with the hope that the American ambassador would arrange their presentation at the Court of St. James's. Fully expecting to be granted this

26

favor, she bought elaborate gowns for the event. One day she ran into Julie Bennett on the streets of London and invited Julie to her hotel room to see the lavish purchases. Julie thought the dresses came closer to looking like Christmas trees in full regalia than any she had ever seen. She privately wondered if the King's eyes might not pop out; but His Royal Highness never had to test his control. The ambassador refused Mag's suit.

This did not prevent Maggie from claiming she had been presented at court in places where she could get away with it. The former waitresses of the Mark Twain Hotel in Hannibal still tell of her marvelous descriptions of royalty and palace pageantry. In the Newport *Social Index* she recorded under "Memberships" the following: Denver Country Club (which was true) and the National Society of Colonial Daughters. (At no time in our history has there ever been any such organization).

Maggie's quick wit was not always spurious. One tale that bears repeating concerns the time she was most anxious to capture one of the leading bachelors of the Newport colony for a dinner party. As an inducement to obtain his acceptance, she extolled the culinary virtues of her cook.

"Thank you," the bachelor replied coldly. "I have a very fine cook of my own."

A COMMITTEE OF "TITANIC" SURVIVORS

After a quick trip to Denver Maggie was back in New York, May 29, to welcome Capt. A. H. Rostron of the Carpathia with a grateful gift.

27

A GIFT MEDAL

Mag gave the captain, officers and crew of the Carpathia this award which showed the rescue ship as it steamed through stark icebergs toward a small lifeboat, tossing in the sea. Each medal was engraved with the individual's name. The reverse side read: "In recognition of gallant and heroic services from the survivors of the S.S. Titanic. April 15, 1912."

"Splendid!" Maggie replied. "Bring her to dinner, too."

Startled by her gall, the bachelor found himself accepting. He came to dinner and developed into one of Maggie's ardent admirers!

The winter of 1911-12 she spent abroad, part of the time in Egypt where John Jacob Astor had taken his young wife, Madeleine Force Astor. Here they did a bit of sightseeing together and, when the Astors said they were returning to America on the maiden voyage of the great new White Star ship, the S. S. "Titanic," Mrs. Brown determined to try for passage and to sail earlier than she had planned. Because of her frequent trips in former years she was able to get on the sailing list at the last moment.

On that fateful April night when J. Bruce Ismay, chairman of the Board of the White Star Line, wanted to make a record time for an Atlantic crossing, Mrs. Brown was walking on the promenade deck with George A. Brayton, a friend from Los Angeles. The hour was twenty minutes to midnight. Suddenly there was a bump and a lurch as the giant ship hit and scraped along the hidden ledge of an iceberg, submerged in the north Atlantic seas.

At first no one thought the incident was serious, although several passengers, including Mrs. Brown, sauntered around the deck to discover what had happened. She was dressed in a black velvet dress, trimmed in white satin, and a matching long black velvet coat lined with the white. She had

PHILANTHROPIC

This photo was published in 1914 in "Representative Women of Colorado" by James Alexander Semple. He described Mrs. Brown as a woman of large philanthropic interests, tremendous executive ability and known in the social circles of the large cities in America where she was a favorite. He spoke of her "rare bravery" at the time of the Titanic disaster.

on high buttoned shoes with black bottoms and white tops. A deck officer brought news that an iceberg had gashed the hull of the ship but that the Titanic was probably not in great danger because the water-tight compartments could be closed around the damaged area. As a precautionary measure, the captain had ordered that the lifeboats be lowered.

Mrs. Brown decided to go down to her cabin for her sable stole and her jewels. As she descended the stairs, she found pandemonium spreading through the ship. People who had already retired were running about the gangways in their night garb, trying to find out what to do. Most of the stewards were as bewildered as they. Mrs. Brown suggested that they put on clothes before venturing out on deck; but many were too frightened to heed her words and rushed up the stairs in their flimsy garb.

Maggie said later that she wasn't particularly frightened but that she was excited. She had taken $700 out of her handbag earlier in the voyage and hidden it among some lingerie; and this she forgot to pick up. But she did collect her jewels and a travel handbag (which contained a fair amount of money and important papers) in exchange for the dainty one she was carrying. She also picked up a life-belt besides her fur scarf. Then she went back upstairs and out on deck. By then the floor had a definite tilt.

A crisis had developed—it appeared that there were not enough lifeboats to take all the passengers and that the lowering apparatus would not work

PALM BEACH

This was a resort that Maggie liked and visited frequently. She was at the Breakers Hotel in 1925 when it burned down. She escaped with almost nothing. $10,000 was paid for her clothes that were lost. She had many young men friends with whom she danced, but no serious romance.

for some that did exist. One boat's lowering rope had broken or jammed—no one seemed to know which—and dumped all its occupants into the icy waves where they were helplessly swimming about and calling to be saved. The crowds on deck were tense but remarkably orderly. Most preferred to take their chance with the stalwart big ship rather than to brave the discomforts and dangers of the lifeboats. She heard that George Brayton had jumped overboard with a life-preserver. (He survived, despite hours in the icy sea).

"Women and children first!" was shouted as each boat started to load.

Mrs. Brown stood watching at successive loading stations and helping a number of women into boats. She ran into John Jacob Astor and saw him tenderly talking to his pregnant young wife, but neither of them was in any hurry to get into a boat. It was the opinion of many that the Titanic was too well-built and sound to ever sink. Then Maggie moved about the deck to another loading station on the port side and heard Second Officer

30

STRIKING FUR

Maggie liked everything exotic and was particularly fond of all sorts of rare fur. She also liked fancy outfits and to parade the streets, calling attention to her weird get-ups. In Newport she lived opposite a Gentlemen's Club. She loved to entertain the men with hourly promenades. She owned a monkey, too, to show off.

Charles Lightoller call to elderly Mrs. Isidor Straus, who was standing beside her philanthropist husband.

"Here, lady," he said. "There's room in this boat."

"Please give it to someone else," Mrs. Straus replied softly and linked her arm in her partner's. "My husband and I have been together for over forty years and I do not intend that we should be parted now."

By now it was close to one o'clock and Lightoller looked around. Two friends of Mrs. Brown's, Edward P. Calderhead and James R. McCough, who were standing close by, suddenly said:

"Here's a lady."

They swung Mrs. Brown into the boat. Later that week she told the

LATE LOVE

Peggy Shaw, now Mrs. Henry Coe of Cody, Wyo., captured Mag's heart in 1924. In 1927 Mag announced in The Denver Post that she was adopting the little girl. But Peggy's parents politely refused.

New York Times during the course of a long interview that she owed her life to these two men. The number of her lifeboat was 6.

By now the Titanic was tilting at a precarious angle and the ship's orchestra had assembled on deck to play "Autumn," although legend has always said the tune was "Nearer My God to Thee." As Mrs. Brown's lifeboat was waiting to swing out, she took a rosary from her handbag and told a few beads for the figures she saw jumping from the decks to brave the icy seas with nothing but a small life preserver.

When the boatload of women was being lowered toward the sea, they found there was only one seaman among them, to man the oars, as a helper to Quartermaster Hitchens at the tiller. One of the women called back up to the men at the loading station. Major A. G. Peuchen, vice-commodore of the Royal Canadian Yacht Club, offered to swing himself out on the forward fall and slide down the rope into the boat. This he successfully accomplished and proved to be the only male passenger Lightoller permitted to leave that night. On the starboard side the loading officer had a different system—he tried to fill the boats, regardless of sex.

Boat #6 dropped into the sea at 12:55 a.m.; capacity 65 persons, occupants, 28. Their lifeboat was in grave danger of being sucked down by the undertow of the Titanic when she plunged into the sea. Some of the women became hysterical.

"I'll row," Mrs. Brown volunteered, taking off her life belt. "I haven't for years—but I learned when I was a child on the banks of the Mississippi river. I'll bet I still can."

She and Seaman Fleet and Major Peuchen each manned an oar, and Maggie organized two other women for one oar, one to hold it in place and one to row. In this way they swung the lifeboat away from the side of the ship and out into the Atlantic. Seeing Mrs. Brown throw her enormous vitality into the pull of her oar, two other women gained courage and offered to help or substitute when the first tired.

"That's great," Mrs. Brown replied. "And let's sing."

The tilt of the Titanic was fast reaching a forty-five degree angle but the orchestra was still playing its farewell hymn. Mrs. Brown's tremendous, trained voice joined the tune although she had to fake the words. The women in the lifeboat stopped crying and screaming, and the two volunteers added their weight to the oars, calm and determined. The lifeboat moved away to safety.

A short distance out from the Titanic, it became apparent that the figures who were jumping from the decks of the great liner would perish in the cold of the icy seas. The women in #6 wanted to return and pick them up but Quartermaster Hitchens refused. He also refused to row when Major Peuchen suggested that a lady could steer as well as he, while Hitchens put his muscle into a more useful occupation. The quartermaster shouted that he was in charge. In surly silence the occupants of #6 rowed on and finally watched the Titanic sink into the sea at two-twenty in the morning, numbed by the sight as well as the cold.

Trouble with Hitchens increased. His courage failed and he said all was lost. They had neither food nor water, compass nor charts. He declared there was no point in rowing. The women rebelled, and Maggie told him to shut up and row. Later they tied up with #16 and Maggie borrowed a grimy stoker from the other boat to man an oar. Hitchens attempted to stop her. She told him that if he dared touch her, she would throw him overboard. Later Maggie took off her sable stole to wrap around the stoker who was suffering desperately from the cold. Her companions said that this kind act saved the man's life.

About three-thirty in the morning rockets from the S. S. Carpathia proved rescue was steaming into sight. Shortly after four she began picking up survivors of the disaster. Mrs. Brown's boat had drifted, in their effort to keep warm by physical exercise and to reach the light of a ship they saw in the distance, three or four miles away, and its load of people was one of the last to be rescued. It was on the waves six hours, until seven o'clock—but none of its occupants were dead. When the Carpathia's captain could find no more survivors and gave the order to steam southward toward New York, it was eight-fifty in the morning.

The Titanic sank on a Sunday night, and the Carpathia did not dock until Thursday. During this period the lounging saloon of the Carpathia served as a hospital where Maggie Brown spent the whole time, night and day, nursing the sick and receiving messages from the dying to be delivered to relatives back home. Confusion reigned aboard the Carpathia most of this period. It was not an especially large ship, and the addition of seven hundred and five passengers, interlopers with no belongings, made the task of caring for everyone almost impossible.

The wireless office was jammed with incoming inquiries and outgoing messages. It took days for even the newspapers to ascertain a partial list of those who had survived and those who had been lost. Mrs. Brown was especially concerned about young Mrs. Astor and wanted their family doctor sent out on the pilot ship at Sandy Hook so that she would not suffer a miscarriage. After it had been arranged that the doctor would accompany the pilot out to the Carpathia, Mrs. Brown returned to her job in the improvised hospital.

She was worried about the foreign women immigrants from the Titanic who sat, huddled and frightened, unable to understand English, and regarded the world with terror. They had lost their men who were on their way to jobs in a strange, new land. Now the women were even more lost than their husbands and brothers at the bottom of the sea since the women had no money and no way to earn it. Starvation for themselves and the children who accompanied them seemed a sure fate.

Mrs. Brown used her knowledge of French and German and a smattering of other foreign languages to find out if the women had any friends or relatives that she could appeal to for help in the crisis. On board the Carpathia she set out to raise a purse to aid these women over the difficult time facing them when they landed in New York. She posted a notice on the bulletin board and helped organize meetings to discuss the situation. Maggie's goal was $10,000, and she was successful in achieving some $7,000 of this.

J. Bruce Ismay, who got into a boat on the starboard side where the loading rule was not rigidly followed, was one of the men survivors. Feeling ran high against him on board the Carpathia, since his was the largest share of responsibility for the disaster, and he kept out of sight completely. But one day Mrs. Brown encountered him, coming out of the wireless office, according to a story she liked to tell many years later. With flashing eyes she faced him and tossed her head high.

"In Leadville, Colorado, where I come from, you would be strung up on the nearest pine tree," she was supposed to have said and swept past.

The captain of the Carpathia gave unstinted tribute to Mrs. Brown for the help she gave him during these trying days, and the two remained friends for years after. Her heart and her courage brought her unselfishness to magnificent heights—heights as magnificent as those of Leadville, the town she always loved and always went back to.

TWO EGYPTIAN SPHINXES JOINED THE LIONS

In March, 1927, Mrs. Brown returned home from Europe, announcing she might wed the Duke of Chartres; and had a new import for her wall.

When the Carpathia docked in New York, a horde of reporters descended on the survivors, avid for details and anxious to determine exactly who had been lost and who saved.

"Oh," they exclaimed, when they saw Mrs. Brown. "You came through."

"Yes," she replied. "Typical Brown luck. I'm unsinkable."

And ever after that, she was known as The Unsinkable Mrs. Brown, a nickname she gloried in and was happy to see in print.

Mrs. Brown remained on the Carpathia all day Thursday and Friday until three in the morning, refusing to go to a hotel for fear of missing relatives of those who had died and for whom she had messages.

Finally, her task completed, she left for the Ritz-Carlton with the final offer that she would act as god-mother to the most hopelessly orphaned cases. She took with her a young Russian woman who had lost her husband and all of her money and who spoke no English. The two women conversed in German. Along about noon Mrs. Brown turned her charge over to the Russian consul for solution of the young woman's problems.

Maggie wired home for money. Ted Brown was acting as Jim's confidential secretary in Denver at the time and carefully screening appeals. According to Ted, Jim was in Arizona, using the name of Bacon in an effort to dodge Maggie's demands. All during the past week Ted had been receiving wires from the steamship company saying she was lost, she was not lost, she was probably lost, and finally that she was safe. Ted relayed all these to Arizona, and finally also her demand for money. Jim acquiesced, and Ted was empowered to supply her with travel fare.

Maggie Brown's great moment showered over her like sparkling fireworks when she returned to Denver a couple of weeks later. Because the House of Lions was rented, she stayed at the Brown Palace Hotel. (She liked to pretend in her show-off moments that the building was one of Jim Brown's holdings. In actuality the hotel was built by Henry C. Brown, no relation.)

The morning that she reached Denver, her suite was pleasantly filled with newspaper reporters, well-wishers and curiosity seekers, while telegrams and notes were continuously delivered in the hands of pill-capped uniformed bellboys. Mrs. Brown was in her element, the one she liked best, a wide flooding limelight—and her story of the Titanic sinking took on better and more heroic details with each retelling. The literal truth was finally lost.

The quarrel between Hitchens and the women swelled into the proportions of a riot. Maggie was supposed to have quelled this riot with a pistol, usually a Colt .45. Actually she owned no gun and did not know how to shoot. Her kind act, when she wrapped the legs of the stoker in her sable stole, grew and grew until she was supposed to have divested herself of a $60,000 chinchilla coat and all of her clothing down to her corset. Still, even without later exaggerations, she had behaved courageously and was a legitimate heroine.

And then came the accolade for which she had struggled for twenty years! The doors of Denver society's palatial homes swung open, following the lead of Mrs. Crawford Hill, queen of the Sacred Thirty-Six. Mrs. Hill planned a luncheon for an Eastern houseguest of Mrs. George B. Berger, another member of the charmed circle. When the leader of Denver society heard that Maggie Brown had returned to town, she invited the Titanic heroine to share honors at the select affair to be held on the first, May Day.

The Unsinkable Mrs. Brown held her breath when her hired hansom cab turned into the short driveway and through the high iron gates. This white stone mansion on the corner of Sherman and Tenth Streets represented the pinnacle of all that she had wanted when she had stepped from the D. & R. G. train, a raw but handsome waitress and an almost illiterate 'teen-ager, into booming Leadville. The tall dreams that ran through her young head, those many years before, had finally reached their fulfillment when she was forty-four.

The Unsinkable Mrs. Brown was too excited, as she sat down at her hostess' right in Mrs. Hill's white and gold dining-room, to analyze this moment of success. All she knew was that she was floating on clouds as foamy as the white flowers in the centerpiece.

MAG PULLED A FAST ONE ON THE DENVER POST

This painting, borrowed from Mrs. Horace Bennett, she had photographed and in 1929 palmed off as a picture of herself in a Sarah Bernhardt role. She laughed to Mrs. Bennett over her clever trick.

But there were others who could; and they pointed out that so long as Maggie Brown attempted to storm the citadel of Denver society with selfish bludgeoning and sounding brass, she got nowhere. But when she completely forgot herself in the service of the many unfortunates of the Titanic disaster, she received her reward.

* * *

It would be nice to say that Mrs. Brown maintained the prestige of this high point in her life ever afterward. But, unfortunately, she did not. As she grew older, her pretentiousness grew into a disease and her spendthrift ways got completely out of hand. Mrs. Aimee Reitz, owner of the Newport cottage which Mrs. Brown rented from 1913 to 1922, brought action against Maggie for trespass and ejectment on June 25, 1918. But it was four years before the harassed Mrs. Reitz could recover her property; and whether she ever collected any of the back rent, the records do not say.

Jim Brown died in 1922, leaving no will, and Mag became embroiled in a bitter legal struggle with her son and daughter over the disposition of Jim's estate. In these years she constantly hired and fired new attorneys.

She had moments when her finer impulses held sway but these moments were marred by her desire for publicity and her arrogance and contentiousness.

Long before this she had taken to carrying a staff from time to time, and this habit now became her trademark. She appeared always with either a swagger stick by day or a tall shepherd's crook with evening dress, swinging lustily and calling attention to the pride of her walk. Often her staff was decorated with fresh violets or roses to match the color of her costumes which always affected a lavish use of sweeping plumes or fur. Many curious eyes turned to watch her progress through hotel lobbies in Palm Beach, Havana, Paris, London, and New York. In Denver, where she was a familiar figure, people merely shrugged their shoulders and said:

"Ah, The Unsinkable."

As she grew older, she maintained her imperious manner and her red hair with frequent applications of artificial aid to the latter. But both helped to preserve the illusion of handsomeness which she had possessed as a younger woman.

A rather charming interlude occurred in July, 1924. Mrs. Harry Payne Whitney, who was the sculptress Gertrude Vanderbilt Whitney, had just completed her statue of Buffalo Bill mounted on a horse. The statue was to be unveiled in Cody, Wyoming, during the course of a three-day celebration over the Fourth of July. A special train, bearing Mrs. Whitney's guests, arrived from New York in time for the ceremony and festivities.

Mrs. Brown was in Denver at the time and received a letter from Mrs. Whitney suggesting that she might like to join the party in Cody. Maggie would like nothing better. She quickly caught a train and was quartered with the Ernest Shaws, owners of *The Cody Enterprise*, a young struggling couple who did all their own work.

Effie Shaw was prepared to dislike the pretentious, boastful woman who talked so much about lavish parties she had given or attended. But soon she saw another side, and the two became great friends. Instead of staying three days, Maggie's visit stretched into a week.

"This town with its oil industry is like Leadville when it was young," Maggie said wistfully. "If I were a young man, I would settle down here and invest. It has a great future."

Effie and Ernest were surprised when she said this, because the general belief in Cody at the time was that the big oil boom was over.

"No," Maggie said, "I have a sixth sense of vision. I see great things for the Big Horn Basin and the Oregon Basin."

Time later proved Maggie's vision right.

During her stay Maggie grew to be friends with all the children in the block and particularly with the Shaw's own five-year-old daughter, Peggy. Maggie was always very fine with children—they brought out the best in her, her gayety, her wit and her warmth. She frequently sent the children on

MAGGIE AND THE COAT GREW OLD TOGETHER

In 1927 The Denver Post used the first photo with a write-up of her forthcoming memoirs. Her script later formed the basis for the novel, "The Unsinkable Mrs. Jay," in which Maggie did all the things she wished she had. Fortune Magazine wrote her up with the other in 1930.

errands for her, to mail letters, to buy hamburgers, or to inquire about telegrams. Each time she tipped the child with a silver dollar, and they were all bug-eyed. The largest coin most of them had ever seen was a dime.

She gave Effie a great deal of encouragement; said not to mind being poor with small babies and a lot of work to do.

"That was the happiest time of my life when I was young like you in Leadville, living in a white clapboard house almost like this," Maggie added.

Maggie made herself one of the family and lived at their simple scale, eating corn beef and cabbage. By the time she left, she had mentioned a number of times that she would like to adopt Peggy. She added that she was very bitter about her own family and would like to start over again. She asked for Peggy's picture and for many years sent Peggy gifts, dolls from Paris and other souvenirs of her travels. Maggie's restlessness made her keep moving, ever roving, but her letters went back regularly to Leadville and Cody.

"Good-bye, Effie," she said at the station platform. "I have been very disappointed that money did not bring me happiness but this has been one of the happiest periods of my life."

Several of Mrs. Brown's later accomplishments deserve mention. In 1927 she saved Eugene Field's historic house in Denver to make into a library by a spirited campaign to arouse public interest and to raise money for the project. This included a one-man performance by herself as entrepreneur of an amateur program in the Civic Auditorium. The performance was disastrous but the newspapers reported that " 'The Unsinkable' proved herself worthy of wearing the cognomen in the manner in which she steered the melange through two stormy hours." She also took part in the program by a rendition of several of Eugene Field's poems "that rather startled the audience out of its lethargy." Only one hundred people attended in a hall that seated twenty-five hundred.

She studied dramatic technique under Sarah Bernhardt's former teacher and staged a performance of "L'Aiglon" in France, with herself in the title role. The critics were contemptuous.

Her native generosity always remained an outstanding characteristic. In 1928 she offered to redeem the $14,000 mortgage on the Matchless mine in Leadville when another colorful Coloradan, Baby Doe Tabor, found herself in difficulties and about to lose the mine. But in 1928 Mrs. Brown no longer had any such sum that she could lay hands on—it was a gesture that she could not back up. Her profligacy had brought her almost to poverty.

But her heart was always anxious to help. A few weeks before she died, she visited relatives in Leadville and decided that she must give the town's poor children, made even more destitute by the depression of the 1930's, a really fine Christmas. When she returned to New York, she shipped west wool mittens, mufflers, and stout boots which she had previously ordered be strung on an enormous Christmas tree, erected in the middle of Leadville.

Maggie Brown did not live to have her orders carried out, and the Christmas tree was never erected. But nephew Ted Brown quietly distributed the gifts to the town's most needy in her name.

She died October 25, 1932, in the Barbizon-Club Hotel in New York at the age of sixty-five, still a delightful raconteur, but her always fancy clothes now seedy and unkempt. When the *Newport Daily News* printed an obituary which said, "Mrs. Brown was formerly Miss Margaret Tobin, daughter of an Irish peer," more than one reader smiled at what was palpably "another of 'The Unsinkable's' tall ones." To many diners in the restaurants of New York and the cafes of Paris, which she frequented, she was merely a laughing stock.

But to many more, who had known her finer moments, she was always the woman with a "heart as big as a ham," a vigorous relic of Leadville's bonanza days.

A VERY RESTRAINED COSTUME FOR MAGGIE

Generally Mrs. J. J. Brown's taste was florid. She loved lavish adornment both in clothes and in furnishings. This dress is unique for its simplicity when compared to most of her costumes, even though she could not resist having a bunch of flowers tacked to the end of the train. This photo also shows off her small feet of which she was inordinately proud and for which she bought hundreds of costly shoes.

SPECIAL CLOTHES CREATED A SUPERSTITION

*If Maggie had a good time in a dress the first time she wore it, she
would have it made over repeatedly to preserve its good luck charm.
Note that this is the same dress as on page 25 although both her figure and the style of the dress have been much altered in the interval.*

SPLENDOR CHARACTERIZED THE INTERIORS

The House of Lions has already been pictured in the middle spread of this booklet including the dining room, above. There it was viewed from the library and was banked with flowers around a table draped in white linen. Here it is in ordinary garb—if ordinary is the right word. Below is the living room decorated for the same 1910 party as illustrated previously. The floral decorations obscure the furniture.

43

SOME OF MAGGIE'S LOVES WERE SINCERE

Above are pictured Lawrence and Helen Brown, Maggie's children, with their dog, pony and pony cart. All her life Maggie had a real gift with young children. They brought out her finest and most generous side. Below is the Eugene Field house after it had been saved by Maggie's crusade, moved to Washington Park from West Colfax, and been turned into a library. In 1963 it was still serving its high purpose.